Piano Recital Showcase

8 FAVORITE PIECES CAREFULLY SELECTED FOR LATE INTERMEDIATE LEVEL

CONTENTS

ISBN 978-1-4234-5658-2

HAL•LEONARD®
CORPORATION
7777 W. BLUEMOUND RD. P.O. BOX 13819 MILWAUKEE, WI 53213

In Australia Contact:
Hal Leonard Australia Pty. Ltd.
4 Lentara Court
Cheltenham, Victoria, 3192 Australia
Email: ausadmin@halleonard.com.au

For all works contained herein:
Unauthorized copying, arranging, adapting, recording or public performance is an infringement of copyright.
Infringers are liable under the law.

Visit Hal Leonard Online at
www.halleonard.com

Berceuse for Janey

(on a theme by Johannes Brahms)

By Carol Klose

Andante espressivo (♩ = 69-72)

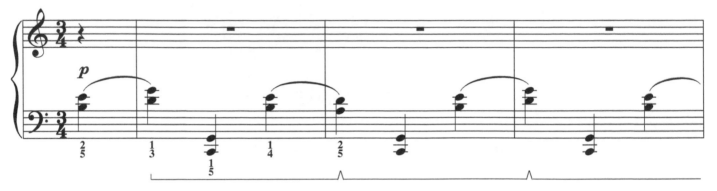

Copyright © 2004 by HAL LEONARD CORPORATION
International Copyright Secured   All Rights Reserved

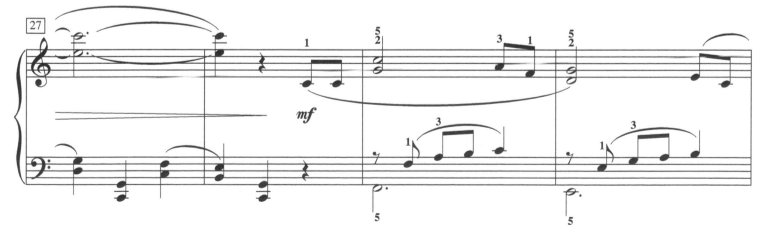

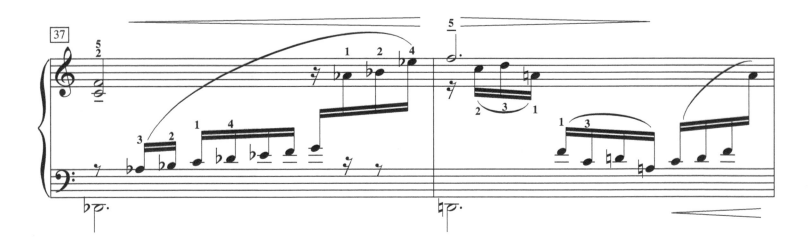

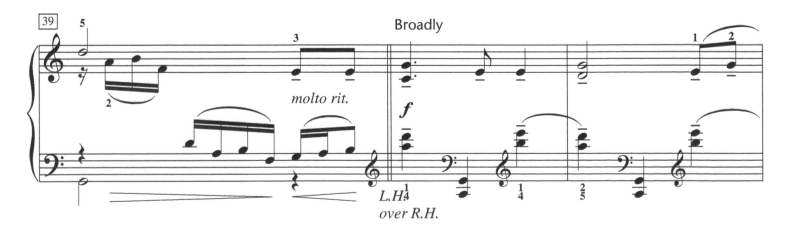

4

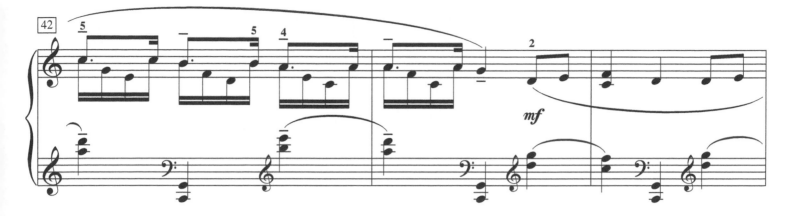

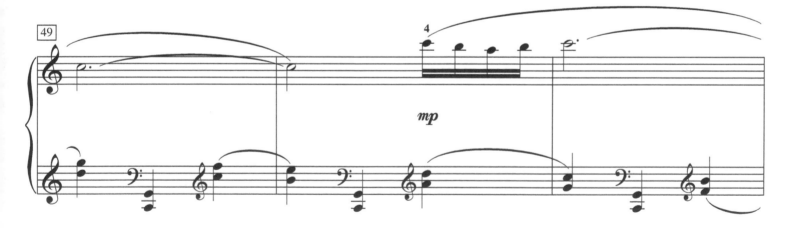

5

Café Waltz

By Matthew Edwards

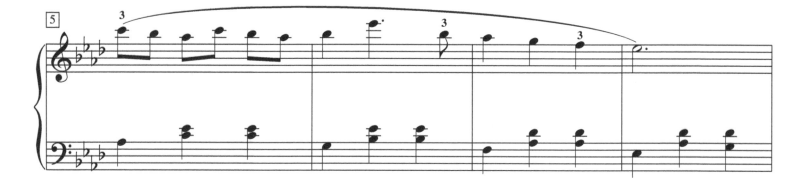

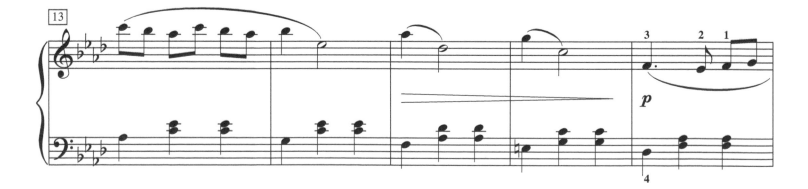

Copyright © 2002 by HAL LEONARD CORPORATION
International Copyright Secured   All Rights Reserved

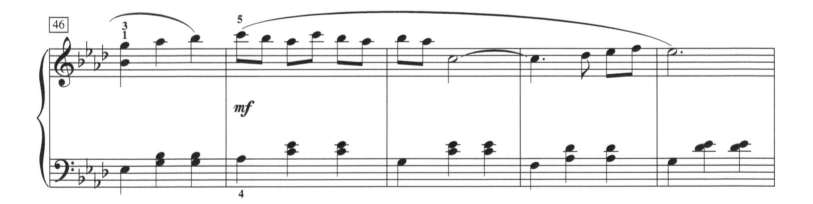

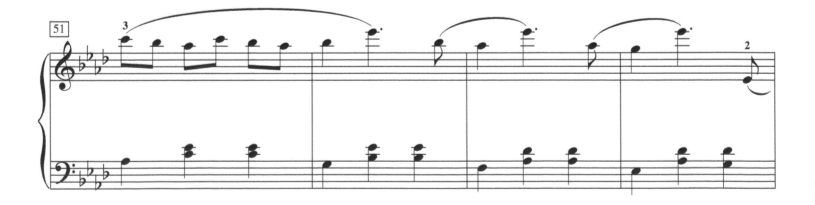

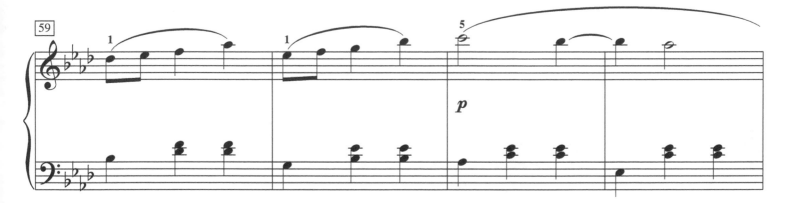

senza pedale

9

Forever in My Heart

By Phillip Keveren

Flowing gracefully ($\quarternote$ = 108-112)

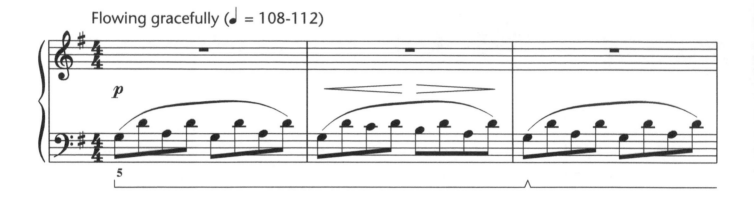

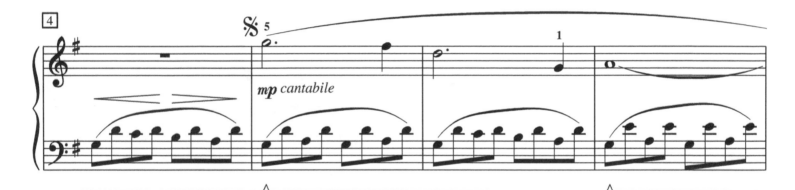

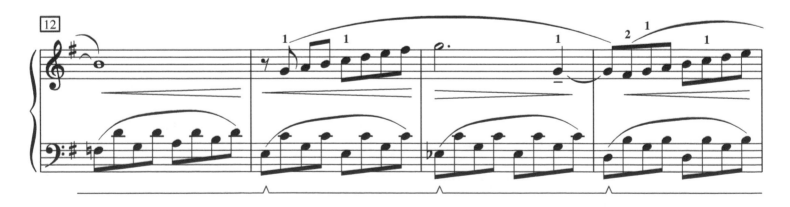

Copyright © 2000 by HAL LEONARD CORPORATION
International Copyright Secured   All Rights Reserved

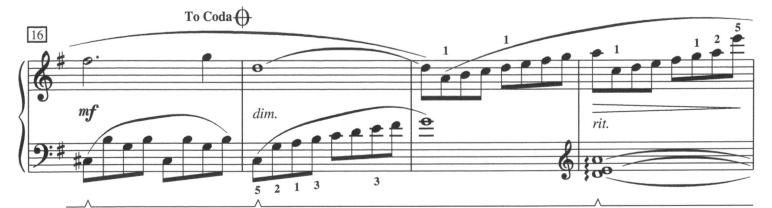

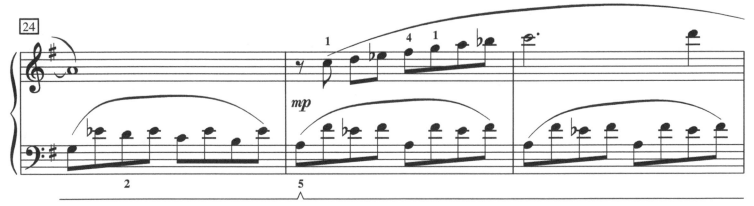

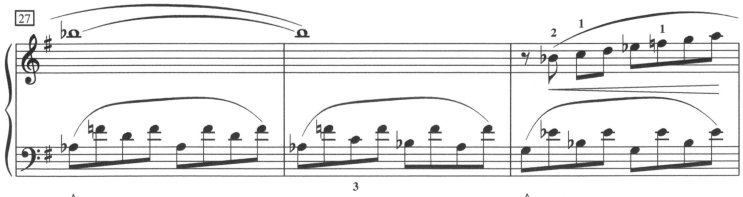

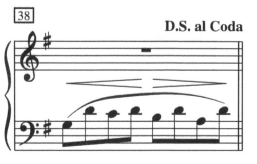

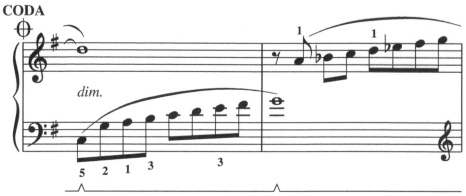

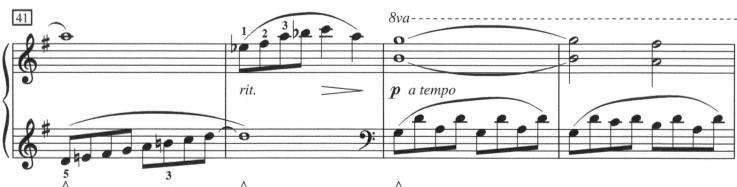

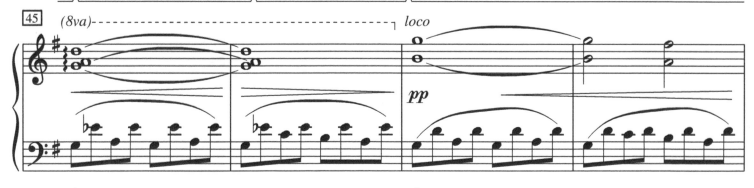

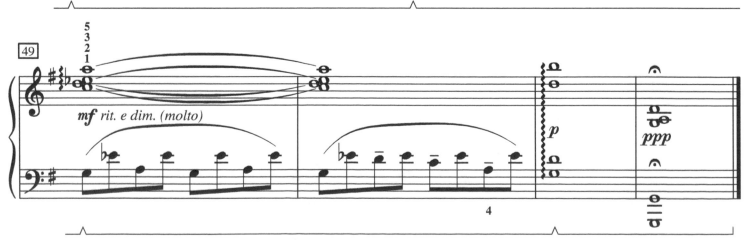

Indigo Bay

By Jennifer Linn

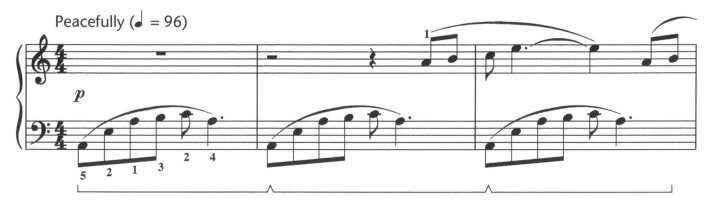

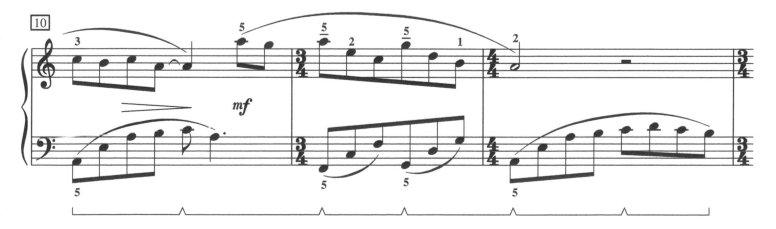

Copyright © 2000 by HAL LEONARD CORPORATION
International Copyright Secured   All Rights Reserved

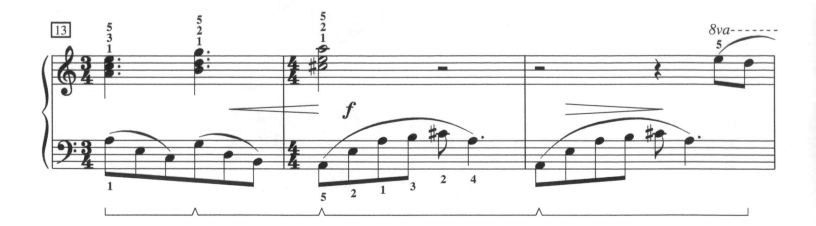

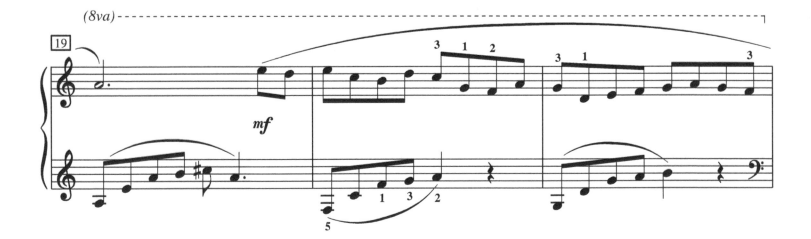

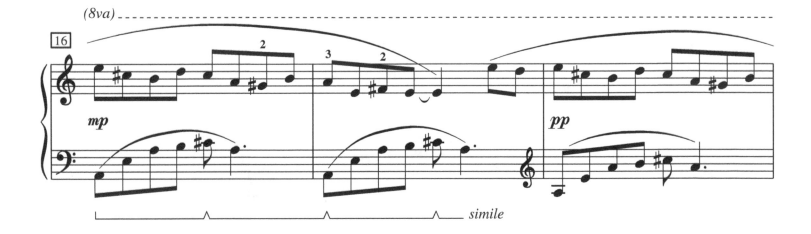

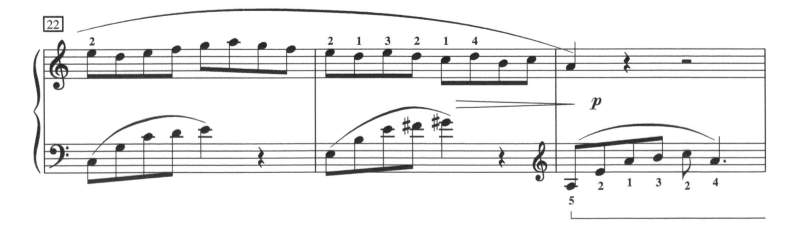

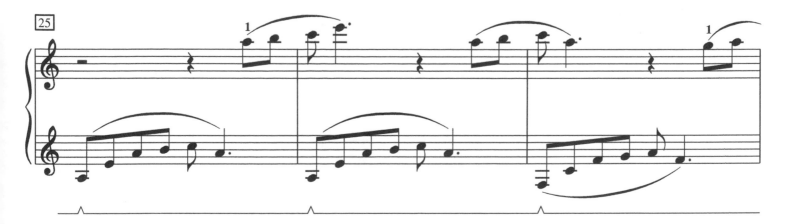

Salsa Picante

By Carol Klose

Allegro ritmico (♩ = 160-176)

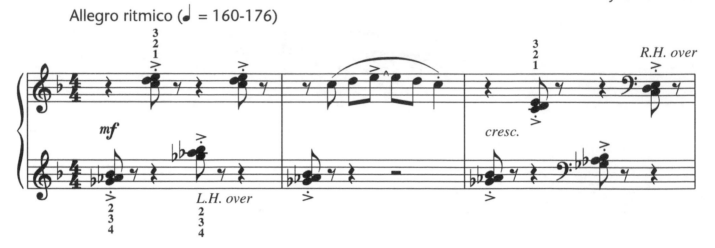

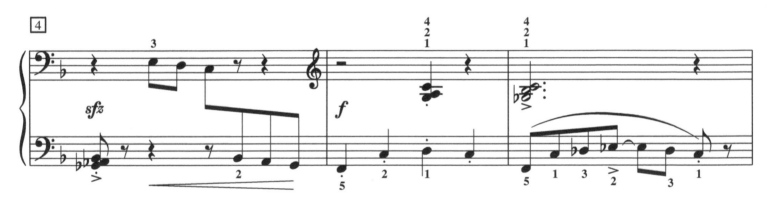

Copyright © 2000 by HAL LEONARD CORPORATION
International Copyright Secured   All Rights Reserved

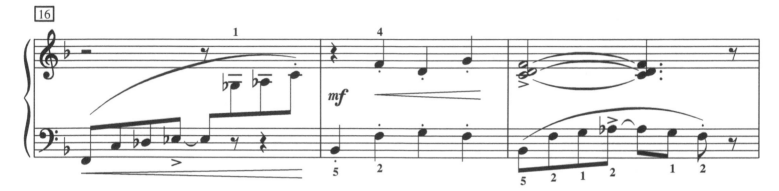

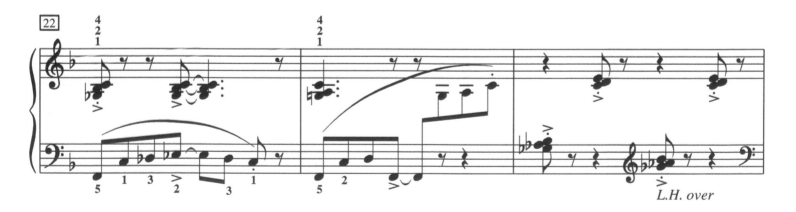

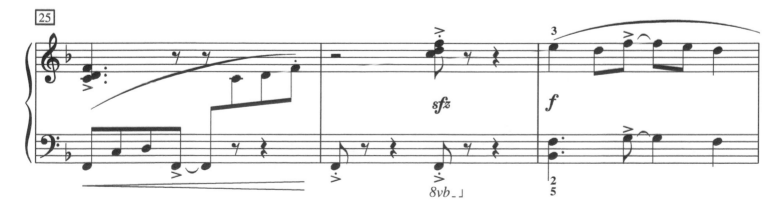

17

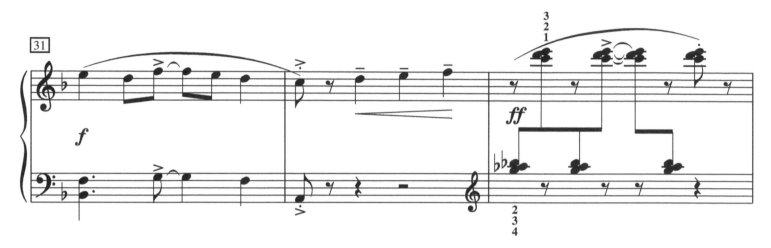

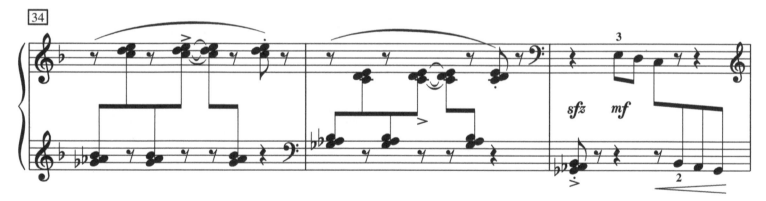

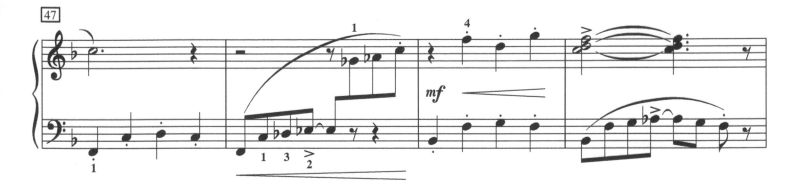

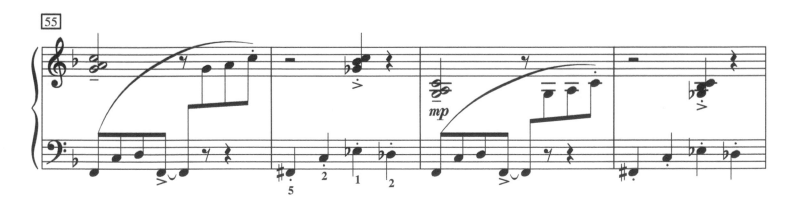

Skater's Dream

By Carol Klose

Flowing (♩ = 138-152)

simile

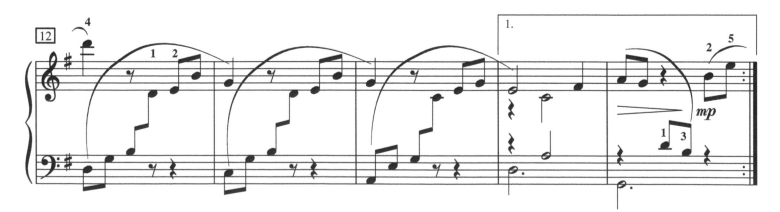

Copyright © 2000 by HAL LEONARD CORPORATION
International Copyright Secured   All Rights Reserved

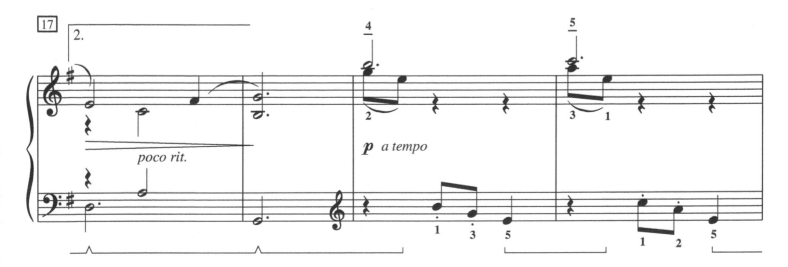

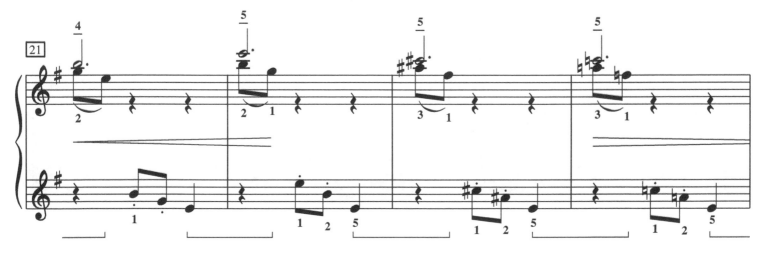

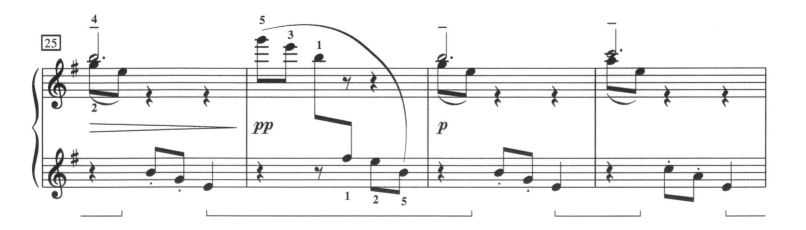

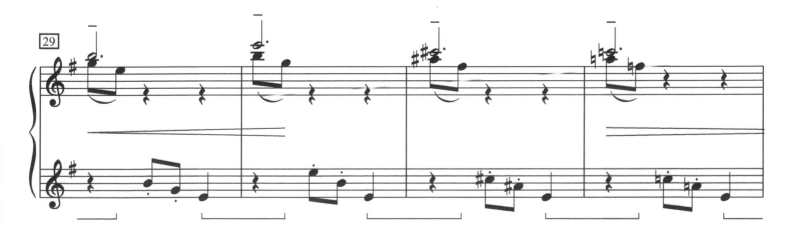

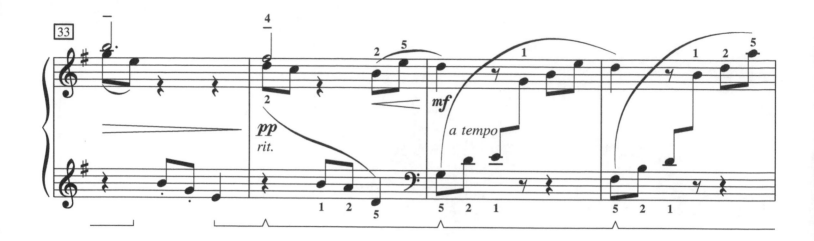

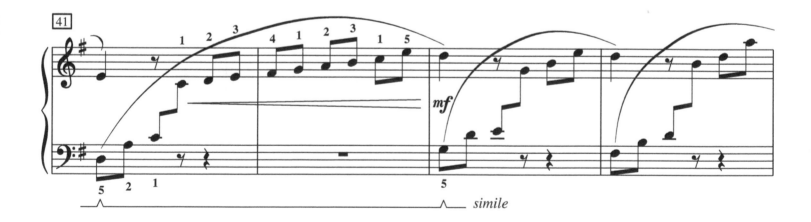

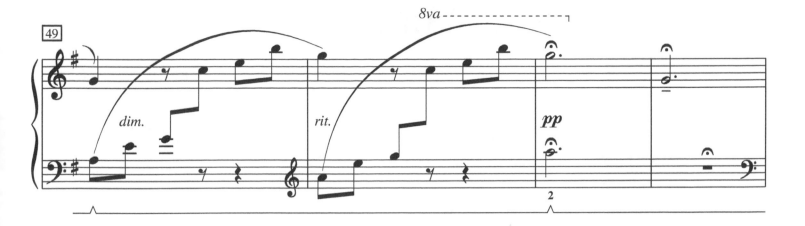

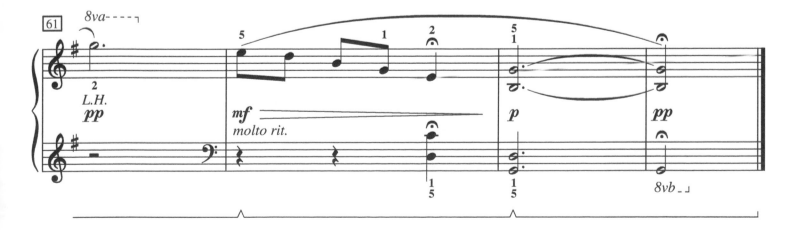

Twilight on the Lake

By Matthew Edwards

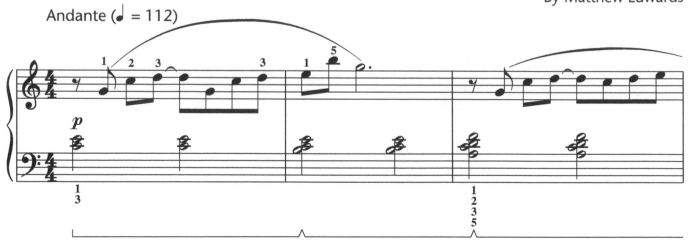

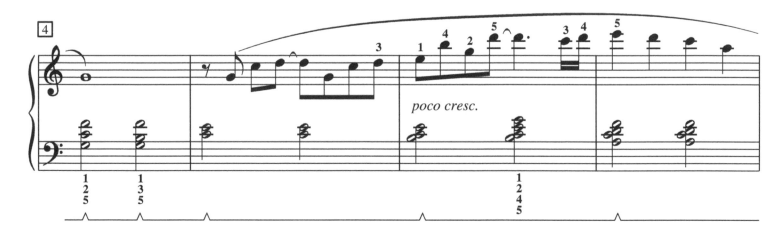

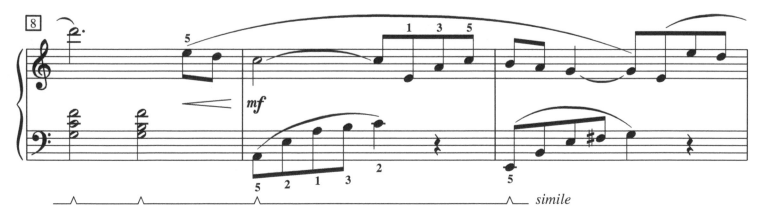

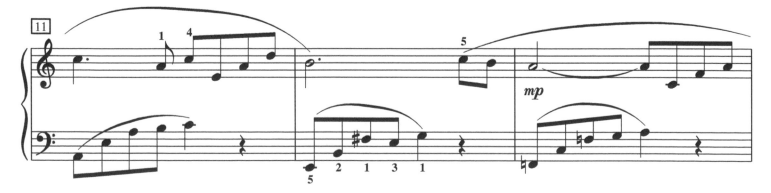

Copyright © 2001 by HAL LEONARD CORPORATION
International Copyright Secured All Rights Reserved

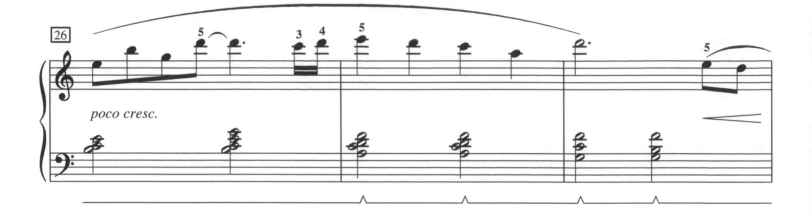

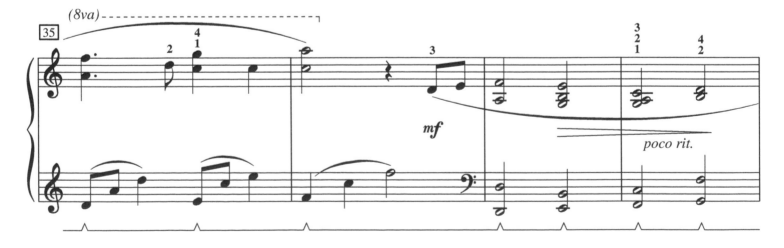

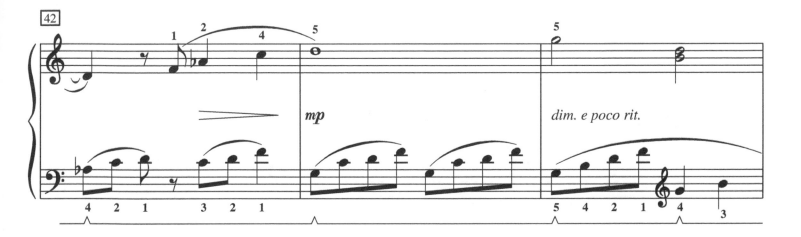

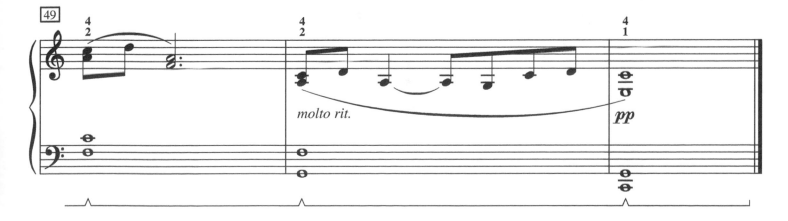

Sassy Samba

By Mona Rejino

Rhythmically, with spirit (♩ = 152-168)

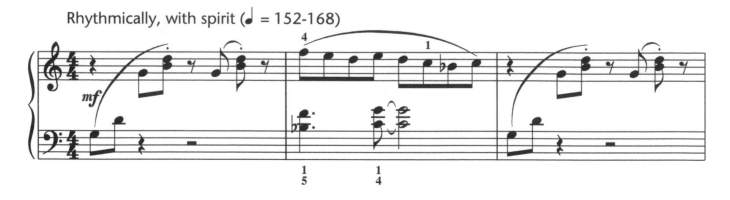

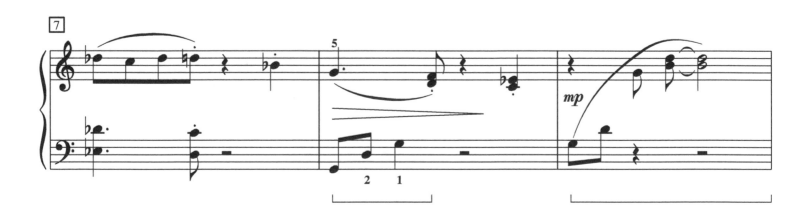

Copyright © 2000 by HAL LEONARD CORPORATION
International Copyright Secured   All Rights Reserved

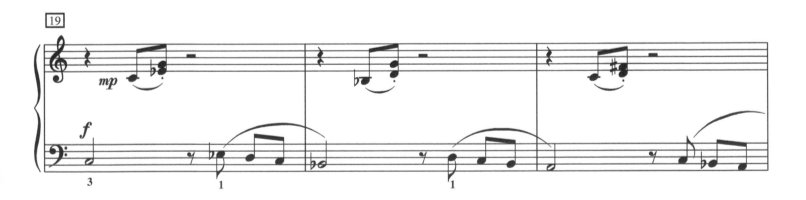

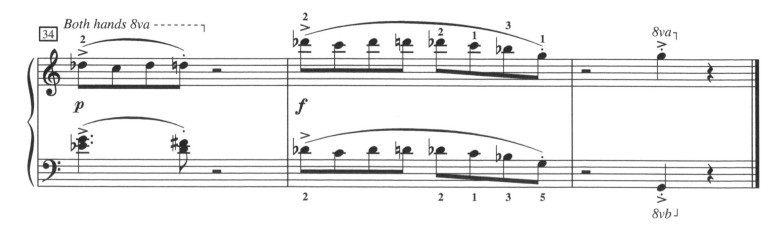

This series showcases great original piano music from our **Hal Leonard Student Piano Library** family of composers. Carefully graded for easy selection.

BILL BOYD

JAZZ BITS (AND PIECES)
Early Intermediate Level
00290312 11 Solos............$7.99

JAZZ DELIGHTS
Intermediate Level
00240435 11 Solos............$8.99

JAZZ FEST
Intermediate Level
00240436 10 Solos............$8.99

JAZZ PRELIMS
Early Elementary Level
00290032 12 Solos............$7.99

JAZZ SKETCHES
Intermediate Level
00220001 8 Solos............$8.99

JAZZ STARTERS
Elementary Level
00290425 10 Solos............$8.99

JAZZ STARTERS II
Late Elementary Level
00290434 11 Solos............$7.99

JAZZ STARTERS III
Late Elementary Level
00290465 12 Solos............$8.99

THINK JAZZ!
Early Intermediate Level
00290417 Method Book............$12.99

TONY CARAMIA

JAZZ MOODS
Intermediate Level
00296728 8 Solos............$6.95

SUITE DREAMS
Intermediate Level
00296775 4 Solos............$6.99

SONDRA CLARK

DAKOTA DAYS
Intermediate Level
00296521 5 Solos............$6.95

FLORIDA FANTASY SUITE
Intermediate Level
00296766 3 Duets............$7.95

THREE ODD METERS
Intermediate Level
00296472 3 Duets............$6.95

MATTHEW EDWARDS

CONCERTO FOR YOUNG PIANISTS
FOR 2 PIANOS, FOUR HANDS
Intermediate Level Book/CD
00296356 3 Movements............$19.99

CONCERTO NO. 2 IN G MAJOR
FOR 2 PIANOS, 4 HANDS
Intermediate Level Book/CD
00296670 3 Movements............$17.99

PHILLIP KEVEREN

MOUSE ON A MIRROR
Late Elementary Level
00296361 5 Solos............$8.99

MUSICAL MOODS
Elementary/Late Elementary Level
00296714 7 Solos............$6.99

SHIFTY-EYED BLUES
Late Elementary Level
00296374 5 Solos............$7.99

CAROL KLOSE

THE BEST OF CAROL KLOSE
Early to Late Intermediate Level
00146151 15 Solos............$12.99

CORAL REEF SUITE
Late Elementary Level
00296354 7 Solos............$7.50

DESERT SUITE
Intermediate Level
00296667 6 Solos............$7.99

FANCIFUL WALTZES
Early Intermediate Level
00296473 5 Solos............$7.95

GARDEN TREASURES
Late Intermediate Level
00296787 5 Solos............$8.50

ROMANTIC EXPRESSIONS
Intermediate to Late Intermediate Level
00296923 5 Solos............$8.99

WATERCOLOR MINIATURES
Early Intermediate Level
00296848 7 Solos............$7.99

JENNIFER LINN

AMERICAN IMPRESSIONS
Intermediate Level
00296471 6 Solos............$8.99

ANIMALS HAVE FEELINGS TOO
Early Elementary/Elementary Level
00147789 8 Solos............$8.99

AU CHOCOLAT
Late Elementary/Early Intermediate Level
00298110 7 Solos............$8.99

CHRISTMAS IMPRESSIONS
Intermediate Level
00296706 8 Solos............$8.99

JUST PINK
Elementary Level
00296722 9 Solos............$8.99

LES PETITES IMAGES
Late Elementary Level
00296664 7 Solos............$8.99

LES PETITES IMPRESSIONS
Intermediate Level
00296355 6 Solos............$8.99

REFLECTIONS
Late Intermediate Level
00296843 5 Solos............$8.99

TALES OF MYSTERY
Intermediate Level
00296769 6 Solos............$8.99

LYNDA LYBECK-ROBINSON

ALASKA SKETCHES
Early Intermediate Level
00119637 8 Solos............$8.99

AN AWESOME ADVENTURE
Late Elementary Level
00137563 8 Solos............$7.99

FOR THE BIRDS
Early Intermediate/Intermediate Level
00237078 9 Solos............$8.99

WHISPERING WOODS
Late Elementary Level
00275905 9 Solos............$8.99

MONA REJINO

CIRCUS SUITE
Late Elementary Level
00296665 5 Solos............$8.99

COLOR WHEEL
Early Intermediate Level
00201951 6 Solos............$9.99

IMPRESIONES DE ESPAÑA
Intermediate Level
00337520 6 Solos............$8.99

IMPRESSIONS OF NEW YORK
Intermediate Level
00364212............$8.99

JUST FOR KIDS
Elementary Level
00296840 8 Solos............$7.99

MERRY CHRISTMAS MEDLEYS
Intermediate Level
00296799 5 Solos............$8.99

MINIATURES IN STYLE
Intermediate Level
00148088 6 Solos............$8.99

PORTRAITS IN STYLE
Early Intermediate Level
00296507 6 Solos............$8.99

EUGÉNIE ROCHEROLLE

CELEBRATION SUITE
Intermediate Level
00152724 3 Duets............$8.99

ENCANTOS ESPAÑOLES (SPANISH DELIGHTS)
Intermediate Level
00125451 6 Solos............$8.99

JAMBALAYA
Intermediate Level
00296654 2 Pianos, 8 Hands............$12.99
00296725 2 Pianos, 4 Hands............$7.95

JEROME KERN CLASSICS
Intermediate Level
00296577 10 Solos............$12.99

LITTLE BLUES CONCERTO
Early Intermediate Level
00142801 2 Pianos, 4 Hands............$12.99

TOUR FOR TWO
Late Elementary Level
00296832 6 Duets............$9.99

TREASURES
Late Elementary/Early Intermediate Level
00296924 7 Solos............$8.99

JEREMY SISKIND

BIG APPLE JAZZ
Intermediate Level
00278209 8 Solos............$8.99

MYTHS AND MONSTERS
Late Elementary/Early Intermediate Level
00148148 9 Solos............$8.99

CHRISTOS TSITSAROS

DANCES FROM AROUND THE WORLD
Early Intermediate Level
00296688 7 Solos............$8.99

FIVE SUMMER PIECES
Late Intermediate/Advanced Level
00361235 5 Solos............$12.99

LYRIC BALLADS
Intermediate/Late Intermediate Level
00102404 6 Solos............$8.99

POETIC MOMENTS
Intermediate Level
00296403 8 Solos............$8.99

SEA DIARY
Early Intermediate Level
00253486 9 Solos............$8.99

SONATINA HUMORESQUE
Late Intermediate Level
00296772 3 Movements............$6.99

SONGS WITHOUT WORDS
Intermediate Level
00296506 9 Solos............$9.99

THREE PRELUDES
Early Advanced Level
00130747 3 Solos............$8.99

THROUGHOUT THE YEAR
Late Elementary Level
00296723 12 Duets............$6.95

ADDITIONAL COLLECTIONS

AT THE LAKE
by Elvina Pearce
Elementary/Late Elementary Level
00131642 10 Solos and Duets............$7.99

CHRISTMAS FOR TWO
by Dan Fox
Early Intermediate Level
00290069 13 Duets............$8.99

CHRISTMAS JAZZ
by Mike Springer
Intermediate Level
00296525 6 Solos............$8.99

COUNTY RAGTIME FESTIVAL
by Fred Kern
Intermediate Level
00296882 7 Solos............$7.99

LITTLE JAZZERS
by Jennifer Watts
Elementary/Late Elementary Level
00154573 9 Solos............$8.99

PLAY THE BLUES!
by Luann Carman
Early Intermediate Level
00296357 10 Solos............$9.99

ROLLER COASTERS & RIDES
by Jennifer & Mike Watts
Intermediate Level
00131144 8 Duets............$8.99

www.halleonard.com

Prices, contents, and availability subject to change without notice.

0321